THE ULTIMATE
CODE-BREAKER'S
PUZZLE BOOK

Dr. Gareth Moore

CONTENTS

WELCOME CODE-BREAKER!

The time has come to put on your best detective hat and try your hand at cracking some secret codes. Have you got what it takes to reveal hidden messages and become a master code-breaker?

Feeling stuck? Don't worry! Turn to the <u>hints</u> section (pages 66-73) for some useful advice to help you along.

Keep a notebook on hand to help you decode the puzzles and jot down the answers to each code you crack. You may also find tracing paper useful for solving some of the puzzles.

Once you have cracked the codes in this book, you can use the methods you have learned to write your own secret messages and codes! Will your friends be smart enough to decode them?

CODE-BREAKER PUZZLES

Welcome Code-breaker, it is time to test your skills!

1

Your first challenge is to examine the flyer below for a secret message. Look for any words that stand out from the rest!

LET'S GO ON AN

Adventure

Whenever you have the chance to go to the beach, do you find yourself carrying lots of heavy bags down onto the sand? If so, then problem solved! The new Beach Master 2000 will be the first thing you pack from now on, since it makes carrying all those beach toys and towels so much easier. Check out our website, and don't forget to use the discount code below.

Up to **30%** off

C0D3-BR3Ak3R-2000

In the text below, some of the letters have been made to stand out from the others. Can you work out which letters these are, and then gather them all together to reveal a secret word?

Capital letters are, Of course, really important. Not only do they Give a clue to where each sentence starts, but they also help make the text easier to Read. All it takes is for you To Use an uppercase Letter instead of a lowercase one. Amazing, isn't it? That's really all it takes. It is so simple and, Of course, it is Never Suspicious.

Master code-breakers hide secrets in all kinds of ways, so always look for suspicious text that might conceal a sneaky message!

Code-breakers Guide

The following scrap of paper, covered in strange symbols, has just been slipped under your door. Can you work out what they mean?

One side looks like this:

♀✳⊕♂♂ ♄✳ ♄♂♂♂ ♂✳♄♂♂♂

♈♂☽♀ ♀♂♂☿

Hmm . . . what on earth could these symbols mean? Perhaps there is a clue on the back.

The other side of the scrap of paper looks like this:

⊕✳♆♄♂♂   MOUTH

♀♀♂♂♈   CREW

♂♂☽♀☿   LEAD

4

You follow the instructions that you decoded from the scrap of paper, and meet your contact at the secret location. To your surprise, they simply pass you a postcard and then leave.

You take a look at the postcard. There doesn't seem to be anything special about the picture on the front, although you do notice some letters and numbers:

A – 1
B – 2
C – 3
X – 24
Y – 25
Z – 26

25 15 21 18
3 15 14 20 1 3 20
9 19
10 1 13 5 19

Code Breaker
3 Spy Lane
Se cr3t

On the back of the postcard are a series of mysterious numbers. **Whatever could they mean?**

5

Your contact must be a master code-breaker! You'd better brush up on some well-known codes. Let's start with the Radiotelephony Spelling Alphabet.

The Radiotelephony Spelling Alphabet replaces each letter with a word, so you can clearly spell out words when saying them out loud. It works like this:

A - Alfa
B - Bravo
C - Charlie
D - Delta
E - Echo
F - Foxtrot
G - Golf
H - Hotel
I - India
J - Juliet
K - Kilo
L - Lima
M - Mike
N - November
O - Oscar
P - Papa
Q - Quebec
R - Romeo
S - Sierra
T - Tango
U - Uniform
V - Victor
W - Whiskey
X - X-ray
Y - Yankee
Z - Zulu

What does the following secret message say?

Lima India Sierra Tango Echo November

Foxtrot Oscar Romeo

Sierra Echo Charlie Romeo Echo Tango Sierra

Now it is time to learn some Morse code! Morse code is a common way of sending messages using sound or light.

Morse code uses a mix of two different sounds or light flashes, known as "dots" (for a short sound or flash) and "dashes" (for a long sound or flash).

When writing Morse code on paper, it is easiest to use a literal dot and dash: ● and –

A . –
B – . . .
C – . – .
D – . .
E .
F . . – .
G – – .
H . . . .
I . .
J . – – – –
K – . –
L . – . .
M – – –
N – .
O – – –
P . – – .
Q – – . –
R . – .
S . . .
T –
U . . –
V . . . –
W . – –
X – . . –
Y – . – –
Z – – . .

Can you decode the following message?

– –

– . – .   – – –   . – .   . . .

– . .   – . – .   – – .   . . .   .

– . .   – . – .   . . .   .

– –   .

–   . .   .

–

– . – –

The following day, a mysterious envelope arrives in the mail. Where there would usually be a postage stamp, however, there is the following picture:

This grid contains a hidden message. **Can you work out what it is?** Can you follow what is going on?

Code Breaker
3 Spy Lane
Se cr3t

PAR AV
air mail

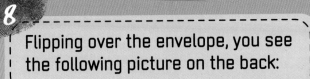

Flipping over the envelope, you see the following picture on the back:

It is another line-based code, but this time using arrows. **What could it mean?** Perhaps the arrows need to be followed in a specific order?

You tear open the envelope and find a bundle of papers.
The first is a letter. Perhaps it contains a hidden message.

I have been having the best summer ever! Will you be joining me? Never again will you have the chance to taste this amazing ice cream, if you don't come! Use your holiday allowance to come and visit. The sea air is incredible, and the beach is wonderful. Same as always, I'm staying in a little cottage just by the sea. Code for the door is also unchanged, making sure you take only the first words. Twice I've asked you to visit now, so please come soon!

IY SO

DP

Hmm . . . eight blank spaces at the bottom. What could they be for? What are there eight of in the letter? Is this a clue?

On the inside of the envelope a short extra note has been scrawled:

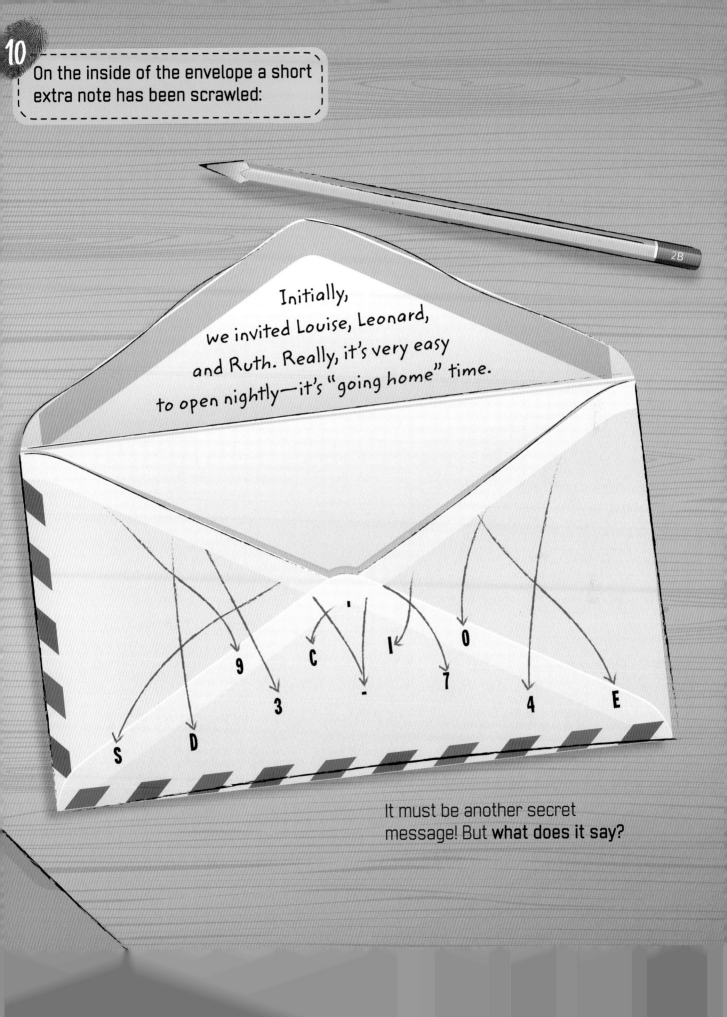

Initially,
we invited Louise, Leonard,
and Ruth. Really, it's very easy
to open nightly—it's "going home" time.

It must be another secret message! But **what does it say?**

Beneath the letter you find two scraps of paper, each with a 3 × 3 grid on it. Some of the grid squares are empty, while others contain letters, or parts of letters.

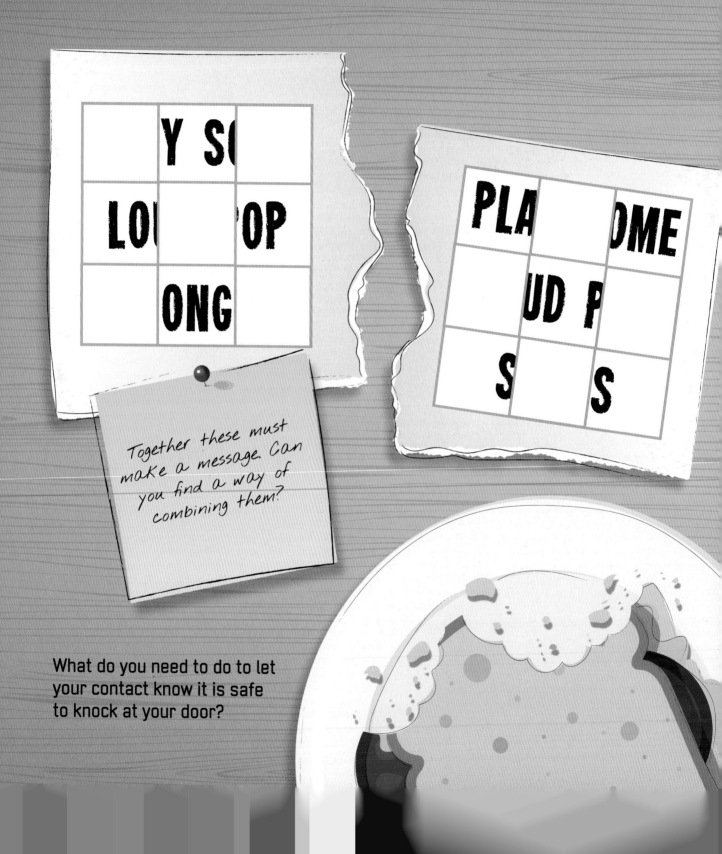

Together these must make a message. Can you find a way of combining them?

What do you need to do to let your contact know it is safe to knock at your door?

All that remains in the envelope now are two more pieces of paper, which once again have grids on them, although now they are 4 x 4:

Code Br
3 Spy La
3+

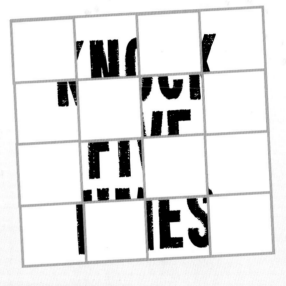

This must be another message from your contact. Perhaps it tells you how they will let you know that they have arrived?

What does it say?

Your contact has arrived and dropped off a mysterious locked box. Stuck to the outside are three patterns, each of which seems to correspond to one of three number dials on the box:

What is the three-digit combination for the lock? You will have to think about how each of these images could be rearranged to make a digit.

The lock pops open, but inside is another box! It also has a three-dial code to solve, but this time it uses letters instead of numbers. There are also three more patterns, similar to those on the previous box:

These patterns must work the same way as the previous code.
What is the three-letter combination for the lock?

You have finally opened the box. What could be so important that it requires all this secrecy? Inside is a page that seems to have been torn from a newspaper.

Friends, we must **reverse the system!** It is the only way to make progress. **What was first must become first.** And not only this: **if you were second, you must now be second to last; and if you were second from last, you should become second.** It is only in this way that we can reveal the truth that has been promised to us!

Xlmtizgfozgrlmh, uirvmw!
Blf ziv mvziob gsviv.
Qfhg lmv urmzo gzhp ivnzrmh.

The second part of this article seems to be nonsense. Whatever could it mean?

Perhaps there is a clue hiding in the first paragraph of the article.

16

Is that really it? You take another look inside the box and are relieved to find a loose scrap of paper. It has a handwritten message on it.

I dropped my keys down the well! Luckily, I am nearly done. This is my last message to you. Finally, I have sent you everything that I have. Once this is decoded, then it will all have been completed. Just take my last word on everything—yes, on it all! Then, with these last words, you have finished this series of tasks.

The "last message"? What could the final code involve? Is there a clue in the text itself?

Can you crack the final code?

SAFE-CRACKER PUZZLES

Time to test your safe-cracking skills! You are on a mission to retrieve ten diamonds stolen by a master jewel thief. Your investigation has led you to a mysterious mansion, where you should find the diamonds hidden inside a series of safes.

1

The first safe is in the entrance hall. To unlock it, you will need to discover the secret three-digit number.

Below the safe, on the floor, is a scrap of paper. It could be a clue, but it seems to contain too many numbers to be useful.

Can you make sense of all the numbers to reveal the correct three-digit number to unlock the safe?

· 2   · 9   · 8   · 18   · 17
· 1
· 10   · 7   · 19
· 16

· 15
· 11   · 6
· 4   · 3   · 12   · 5   · 14   · 13

You've opened the safe to find a security box inside, locked with a five-number padlock. You are sure the first diamond is inside. Perhaps there is another puzzle clue nearby?

Printed on the back of the clue you have just solved, you find a maze. **Could this provide the five-digit number that you need?**

you enter the dining room, where you find a grid of words on the table, to another safe. Maybe the jewel thief left it there as a reminder.

You are used to deciphering the hints people leave themselves in case they forget a combination. You have tried reading this one, but it doesn't seem to make much sense.

Perhaps you only need to read some of the words?

THE	SAFE	CONTAINS	MY	SECRET	NOTES
ON	CODE	WRITING	IDEAS	THAT	HELPED
ME	FOOL	YOU	WITH	WORDS	SINCE
YOU	NEED	WHAT	IS	NOT	FOUR
ONE	THREE	EIGHT	NINE	TWO	SEVEN

What is the safe combination?

NEED A HINT? TURN TO PAGE 68

manage to open the safe to find yet another security box inside,
his time it has a dial on it. All you have to help you crack the
bination is the following picture, which you found with it.

Look's li
someone h
started to
decode it. Th
first three tur
are already
written in.

Can you work out the rest of the
sequence to open the safe?

e safes require you to turn dials left and
to unlock them. For example, you might
he dial three to the left, two to the right,
o the left, then one to the right, to unlock
it. It can take a lot of turns!

NEED THE SOLUTION? TURN TC

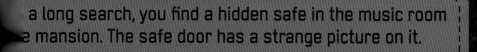

Looking around the room, can you find a clue to help you work out the four-digit combination to the safe?

EED A HINT? TURN TO PAGE 68

Inside the safe is a small box with three dials. Each one can turn to a value from 1 to 6. There is also a picture of a dice face on each dial, but some of the dots seem to have rubbed off.

Could the dice on this shelf help you figure out how to turn the dials?

Can you work out what number each dial should be turned to?

NEED THE SOLUTION? TURN TO PAGE 75

7

You find the fourth safe hidden among the books in the library. It is a particularly complex safe, requiring six digits to unlock it. As you remove it from its shelf, a piece of paper flies out from a book next to it.

0	8	7	2	0	1	7	4	9	4
3	5	7	8	7	3	4	3	9	6
3	4	1	3	7	4	4	2	6	6
9	9	2	7	9	8	4	6	1	8
4	2	2	8	3	5	0	3	6	5
0	8	7	6	6	7	8	7	6	7
7	6	9	6	4	7	0	8	7	3
0	2	2	6	4	6	3	9	8	9
8	7	1	3	7	3	6	8	3	8
7	1	8	5	9	2	8	0	9	7

116470
201749
263789
276984
346729
363447
392646
395888

407087
517370
629479
685739
693437
834783
876616
908295

You are fairly sure that the puzzle you find on the piece of paper could be useful. Which number is different from all of the others in some way?

You type in the six digits, but it turns out this is a two-stage safe. You need another six digits to get to the diamond! What could they be?

You look around and discover another sheet of puzzles on a desk. **Perhaps it holds the key?**

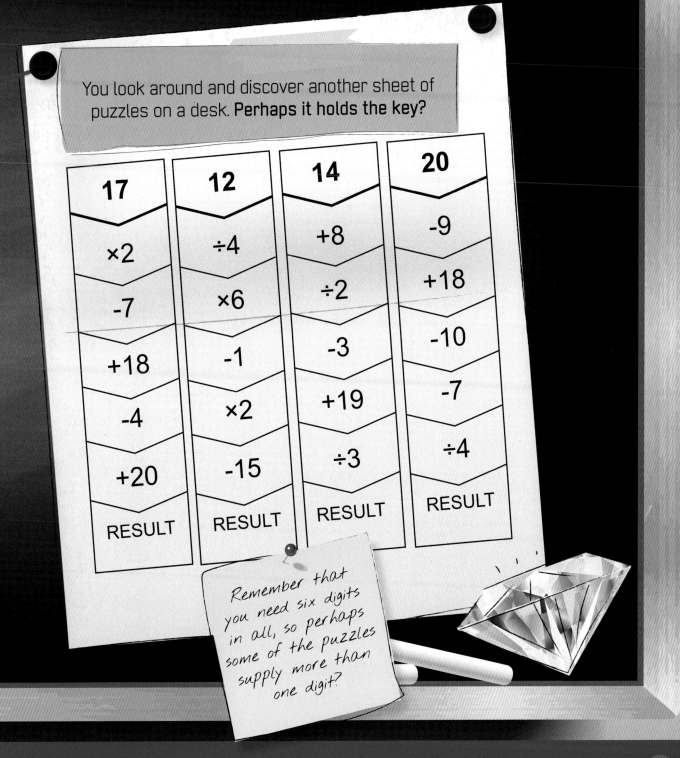

17	12	14	20
×2	÷4	+8	-9
-7	×6	÷2	+18
+18	-1	-3	-10
-4	×2	+19	-7
+20	-15	÷3	÷4
RESULT	RESULT	RESULT	RESULT

Remember that you need six digits in all, so perhaps some of the puzzles supply more than one digit?

NEED THE SOLUTION? TURN TO PAGE 75

g

You go down to the basement and find another safe, but it is proving particularly hard to crack.

You know that you need four numbers, each consisting of two digits. **Can you work out what they are?**

Perhaps something in the basement could offer a clue?

You manage to crack the code, but you find another mini safe inside that requires three digits to unlock.

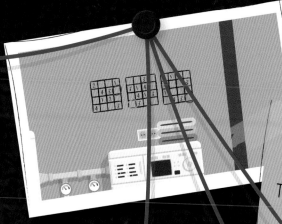

On one of the walls in the basement, you find a series of three drawings. They seem to be different incomplete sudoku puzzles.

Each puzzle has one circled square. Perhaps these squares hold the secret to the safe combination?

Can you work out which numbers belong in the circled squares?

NEED THE SOLUTION? TURN TO PAGE 75-76

11

You find the next safe under the bed in the master bedroom. You are stuck trying to work out the three-digit combination, until you notice the three picture frames on the wall.

Can you figure out the three-digit combination for the safe?

Is there something odd about each set of pictures? Is one image different than all of the others?

Inside the safe you find another lockbox containing one of the diamonds, but it needs a password to open it. You also find a mysterious clear box. There are slots in the top, as if something is intended to be dropped through them.

REHOISNTO

There is a strange model with four bars that came with the clear box. Could this be a clue?

There is also a row of letters inside the clear box. They must be a clue to open the lockbox. **Can you work out what the password is?**

NEED THE SOLUTION? TURN TO PAGE 76

13

In the hallway, you come across a door that is different from the others. Could it be hiding something important? There is a digital display on the door. You need to swipe a particular pattern on the screen, joining together six of the circles in a continuous path.

Luckily, there are numbers in each of the circles. These must act as a clue! **Where and how should you swipe the screen?**

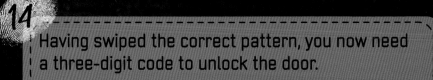

14

Having swiped the correct pattern, you now need a three-digit code to unlock the door.

On the wall next to the door are three sets of images. Could they be a clue? Is there an odd one out on each of the images? **What do you think the three-digit code is?**

1   2   3   4   5

1   2   3   4   5

1   2   3   4   5

You finally gain access to the secret room and find two large display cabinets with the last four diamonds in them. However, they are both locked with a padlock and require a three-digit code to get inside.

On the front of each cabinet is a set of three images. Could these be a clue?

SOB   ZRB

?

SRB   SOF

1. ZRF 2. SOR
3. ZOF 4. SRF

QLP   QAC

?

MLC   MAP

1. QAP 2. QLC
3. MLP 4. MLA

NGY   NGW

?

BHW   NHO

1. NHW 2. BGY
3. BHY 4. BGW

These images appear to be more complex than any you have seen before. Can you crack the three separate codes and then work out which of the options you should choose for each image?

You have managed to get into the first cabinet and retrieve two of the diamonds. There are three more sets of different images on the second cabinet.

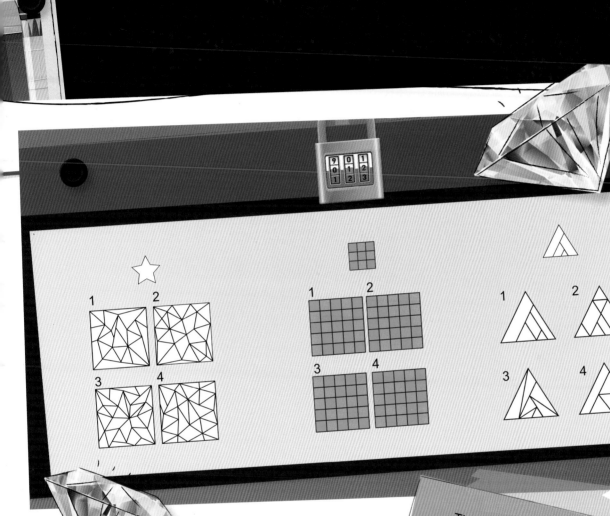

This cabinet holds the remaining two diamonds. What do you think the three-digit code is?

NEED THE SOLUTION? TURN TO PAGE 76

CH DECODER PUZZLES

ks to your master code-breaking skills, you have been hired
cover information from a criminal gang's computer systems.

The first step is to gain access to the system but, when you finally
manage to connect, you are surprised to see that their system
nows the log-in screen not just once but twice.

To access this system please enter the correct passcode. This was
given to you in your introductory "session."

LOG IN

👤 USERNAME

🔒 *********** PASSWORD

Register   Log In

To access the system please enter the log-in password. This is given
to you in your introductory "assignment."

👤 USERNAME

🔒 *********** PASSWORD

Register   Log In

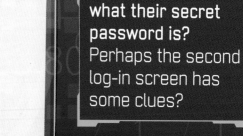

Can you work out
what their secret
password is?
Perhaps the second
log-in screen has
some clues?

EED A HINT? TURN TO PAGE 70

You have logged in with the password, but now you are being asked for a digital identification "key." You have managed to find out that this is represented by the numeric sequence shown below, but the system is refusing to accept it.

IDENTIFICATION KEY:

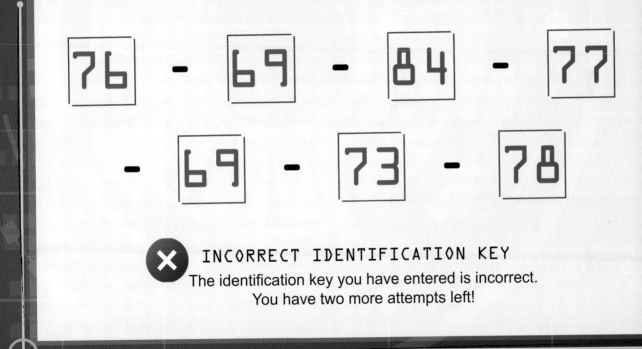

76 - 69 - 84 - 77

- 69 - 73 - 78

✕ INCORRECT IDENTIFICATION KEY
The identification key you have entered is incorrect.
You have two more attempts left!

Perhaps it wants a series of letters instead, but if so then what could these be?

ASCII letter codes

A = 65   G = 71   M = 77   S = 83   Y = 85
B = 66   H = 72   N = 78   T = 84   Z = 90
C = 67   I = 73   O = 79   U = 85   [= 91
D = 68   J = 74   P = 80   V = 86   \ = 92
E = 69   K = 75   Q = 81   W = 87   ] = 93
F = 70   L = 76   R = 82   X = 88   ^ = 94

NEED THE SOLUTION? TURN TO PAGE 77

3

Now you are into the system, you have found some suspicious text files. You feel sure these contain secret information that the criminals want to keep hidden.

Phone calls. Don't forget:

2 555 9 2 999 7777
88 7777 33
2
888 666 444 222 33
33 66 222 666 3 33 777

Add Number

11:33AM   100%

The first file seems to be about the gang's phones. **Can you decode the hidden text?**

4

The next file seems to be more related to numbers, although you feel fairly sure that each of these numbers somehow represents a word.

For each challenge, use the response shown:

BREAKFAST: 77345663

HOLIDAY: 461375

SWIMMING: 5376606

WORLD: 38076

Can you work out what the four challenge responses are?

Hmm . . . maybe we need to look at this code from a different angle?

hEllO

NEED THE SOLUTION? TURN TO PAGE 77

Looking through some of the program code you have found on the computer system, there is an interesting utility file named "secretMaze.code." Could this contain some secret information about the criminals?

```
// Maze creator
// Pay attention to the /*...*/
public class Cell {
public int x;            // x location on plot of map
public int y;            // y location on plot of map
public int f;            /* Whenever accessing */
public int lift;         // lift id, if a floor up/down cell
}

/* our computer systems */
public List<Cell> maze;      // set of all cells in the maze
public List<Weave> weaves;   /* remember to open */
public List<Cave> caves;     // all caves in the maze

/* our identification software */
public void drawMaze {
    foreach (Cell c in maze) {
        drawCell(c); /* so that we can track */
    }
}

// Maze constructor
public Maze(int width, int height)
{
    maze = new List<Cell>(width*height);
    /* all legitimate logins */
    createMaze(maze);
    drawMaze(maze);
}
```

What does it say? You are looking for a 19-word sentence.

6

Interesting. It seems you need to make sure you identify yourself to the system now that you are logged in.

IDENTIFY YOURSELF:

PROVE YOUR IDENTITY:

Perhaps there is something to help you in the file you have just gained access to, which was hidden inside a password-protected archive.

```
           Identification routine
    Remember: one in each pair is a decoy


              QT OX
   IX ED EA NG LT ZI FB DY
   YL OA UP KR SC EW LP FQ
         TJ YJ WP HE
            IZ NZ
   WC UV CX QU LM BZ PE RD
```

NEED THE SOLUTION? TURN TO PAGE 77

Aha, you now have access to some written documents instead of confusing digital code files! Perhaps you are about to find out something really interesting.

Partyinvite.doc

WELCOME TO ALL NEW RECRUITS!

We are delighted to invite you to **our** annual party at the *new* museum in the heart of the city. It will be a wonderful night, because all of our staff and friends from headquarters will be there, along with our field agents, too.

It *is* important to remember that you will be representing the business when in attendance, so make sure that you wear all of your issued kit.

We will see you there, in **Paris!**

This invitation to a party seemed perfectly ordinary at first glance, but then some of it stands out to you. **Could it contain a secret sentence?**

8

Now, this is interesting! You have found two notes attached to that party invitation, and they look the same, but the system is telling you that the files have different contents. Why could this be? Could the pair of notes contain another secret message?

YOUR FILES:

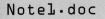 partyinvite.doc   Note1.doc   Note2.doc

Note1.doc

We have changed our plans. Make sure you pay attention to even the smallest of changes.

Usually we have a cleaning team attend every weekday, although not on Fridays.

From next week, this will change and they will attend only on weekends.

The other company that we share the office complex with will no longer be contributing to the cost, so we have decided to reduce our bill.

Please ensure you tidy your desk before the end of each week.

Note2.doc

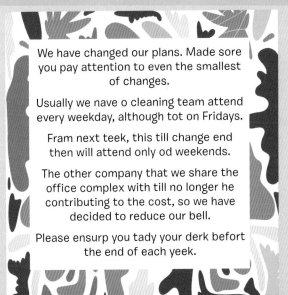

We have changed our plans. Made sore you pay attention to even the smallest of changes.

Usually we nave o cleaning team attend every weekday, although tot on Fridays.

Fram next teek, this till change end then will attend only od weekends.

The other company that we share the office complex with till no longer he contributing to the cost, so we have decided to reduce our bell.

Please ensurp you tady your derk befort the end of each yeek.

NEED THE SOLUTION? TURN TO PAGE 77

This gang are even more shifty than you expected! Many of their coded messages have been hidden in seemingly ordinary-looking files, but now that you are getting deeper into their system, it looks like they haven't worried about disguising the codes at all.

A = B
B = C
C = D

You know the code so you know that:

Sn qdzc sgd mdws bncd, rghes ax sghqsddm okzbdr sgqntfg sgd zkogzads.

Can you make any sense of this document?

NEED A HINT? TURN TO PAGE 71

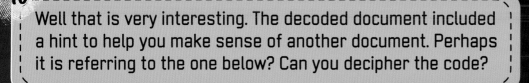

Well that is very interesting. The decoded document included a hint to help you make sense of another document. Perhaps it is referring to the one below? Can you decipher the code?

ABCDEFGHIJKLMNOPQRSTUVWXYZ

Gur cbyvpr ner jngpuvat hf.
Nyjnlf ghea bss lbhe znpuvar jura lbh
yrnir gur bssvpr.

Could this document contain some insider information from the gang?

NEED THE SOLUTION? TURN TO PAGE 77

You have come across some kind of index file, which you think might tell you about the various activities the gang have been up to. As you examine it closer, however, you wonder if it might be a different kind of index.

Find Files...

Index.dat file found:

10: This index file is for keeping track of our main achievements.

10: A copy will always be kept on the central server.

1: Now that we have this facility, we should use it.

5: Server access can be located via the portal link once logged in.

3: Once logged in, make sure not to connect externally.

6: This will otherwise compromise our Frankfurt facility.

OK

CANCEL

There are numbers, but they do not seem to be indexed to pages of the document. What else could the numbers be "indexed" to?
Maybe there is a secret message here?

NEED A HINT? TURN TO PAGE 71

Just after you finally make sense of the previous "index" file, you come across another. Given what you have just learned, you hope this one will be easy! Unfortunately, however, it seems that this file does not use the same format.

75624 9983 652

Find Files...

MainServerPassword.dat file found:

4: Read
1: All
1: Four
8: Insignificant
3: Books
9: Delivered
3: This
3: July

OK

CANCEL

There must be something else you have to do this time. Perhaps it is similar?

According to the file name, it seems it contains the password for the main server. **What is the password?**

NEED THE SOLUTION? TURN TO PAGE 77

You feel that you are getting closer to gaining complete access to the main server, at which point you will be able to hand over everything you have discovered to the people who hired you.

Door1.doc

The following note requires careful alphabetizing. Make sure everything is in the correct order.

CASECS
ORDO
SI
ELBOW
TYPEM
BYEAB

Among the various strange documents you have found, the following note seems to be referring to something the gang are planning to carry out soon. Maybe it contains some information they are passing on to their members? **What does it say?**

 NEED A HINT? TURN TO PAGE 71

Now that you are starting to learn about their plans, you feel that the contents of the file "Door code.doc" is sure to be useful!

Door code.doc

Code jumbled for security purposes:

ETREH
ENNI
VEESN
VEFI
THIGE
ROZE

Does this document contain some kind of door access code? **What is it?**

⚠ SUSPICIOUS ACTIVITY DETECTED

NEED THE SOLUTION? TURN TO PAGE 77

<ytd-masthead id="masthead" slot="masthead" class="shell"
d="disable-upgrade" class="true"><div id="search-container" class="ytd-searchbox-spt"
search-container"> <div id="search-input" class="ytd-searchbox-spt"

15

Aha, you are now into the main server itself. The message that is displayed when you first connected to it seems a little strange, however, with an unusually high number of typing errors.

c-2.7,0.72-4.83,2.85-5.56,5.56C1.45,19.77,1.45,30,1.45,30s0,10.23,1.31,15.13c0.72,2.7,2.85,4.83
,5.56,5.56

C13 ,52,32.88,52,32.88,52s19.66,0,24.56-1.31c2.7-0.72,4.83-2.85,5.56-5.56C64.31,40.23,64.31,3
,64.31,30
S64.31,19.77,63,14.87z"/>
<polygon fill="#FFFFFF" points="26.6,39.43 42.93,30 26.6,20.57"/>

```
      Wecome to the main server. This
      system is fr official use. Do not
          connect for lon sessions.

      Tday's warnings afect all users of
                diferent types.

        Remember: do ot stay lgged
               in afterards.
```

Could it contain another secret warning to gang members? **What does it say?**

16

It looks like they are onto you! There is just time to print out one final document and then you disconnect before your luck runs out.

SYSTEM HACKED

If that luck did last to the final moment, then perhaps this page contains one last secret message? What is it?

irst, we want to say this to you:

ell done on getting this far. veryone thought you wouldn't make it.

Having such a clever person gain access to our systems was really a very large challenge for our smartest experts in computer technology.

Exceptionally good at gaining full systems access as you may be, we carefully concealed all of our most secret and revealing information before your prying eyes first connected. Sorry, but every thing you think you have discovered about us is wrong.

NEED THE SOLUTION? TURN TO PAGE 77

LOCATION TRACKER PUZZLES

Hello, explorer! You are off on an adventure to track down some hidden treasure. You will need to make sense of a series of maps and codes to find your way. Let's start by working on some map-reading skills.

1

For this first challenge, you need to use the letters and numbers at the top of the paper below to trace a path from left to right across the map.

Can you work out the correct path, then trace it with your finger to reveal a symbol that will confirm you are correct?

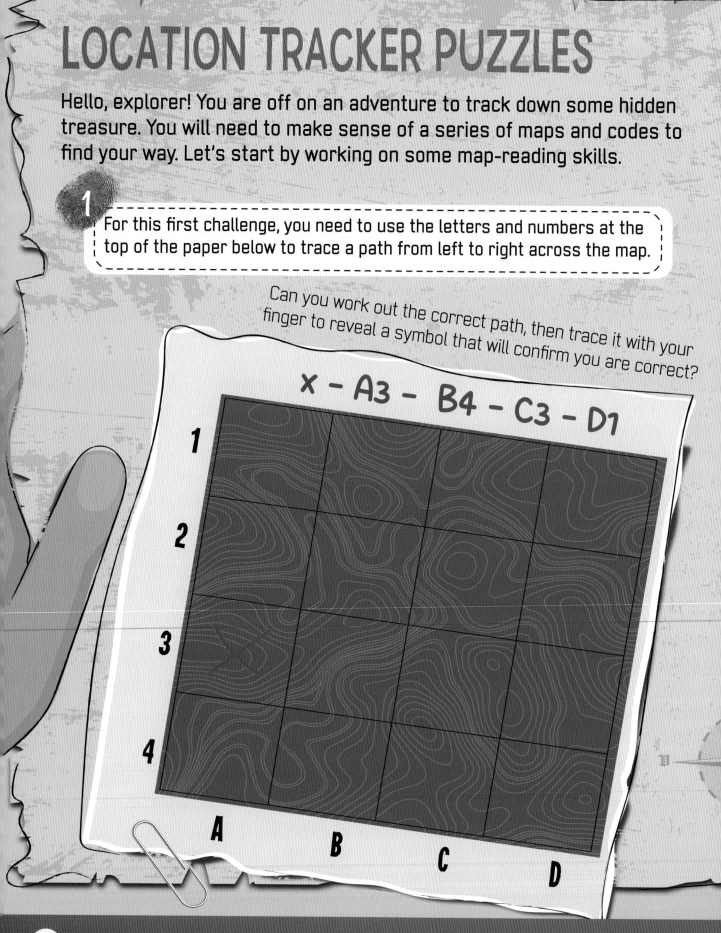

x – A3 – B4 – C3 – D1

1
2
3
4

A   B   C   D

It seems you are a natural map reader! Now it is time to start the treasure hunt, but where should you go first? If you start at the "X" and follow the instructions given, which location will you arrive at?

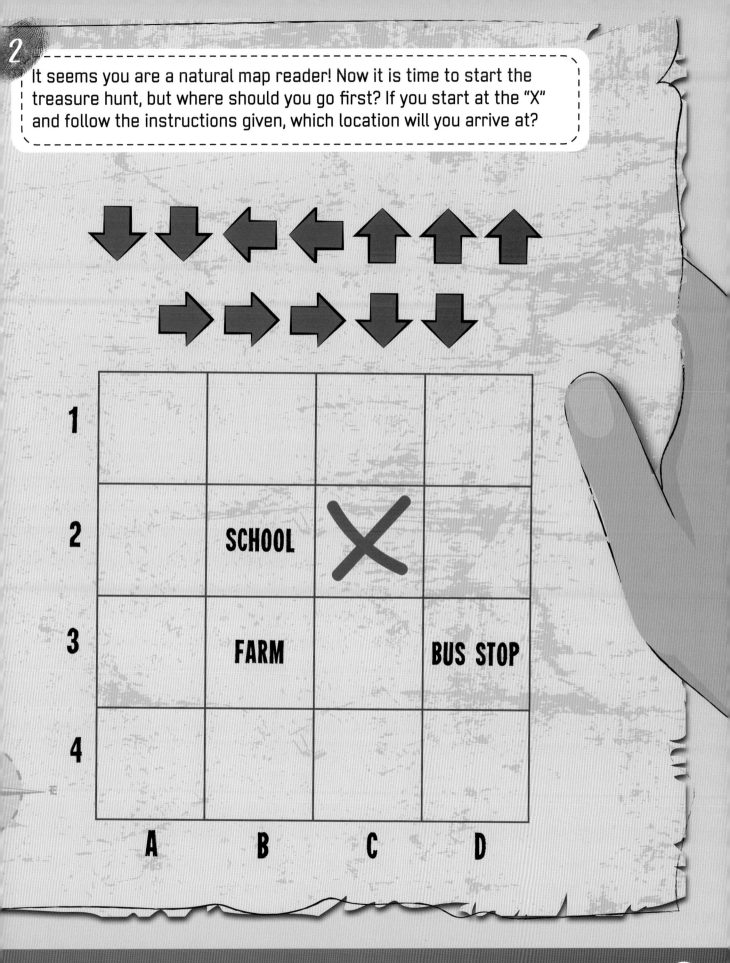

NEED THE SOLUTION? TURN TO PAGE 78

3

You now need your navigational compass, because when you arrived at the start location, you found the following instructions chalked onto the ground:

What could they mean? A map has also been taped to the ground. Can you work out where to go to next?

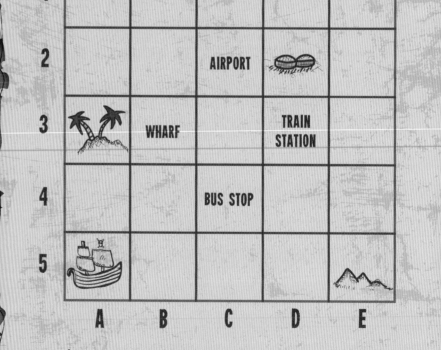

	A	B	C	D	E
1					
2			AIRPORT	✈	
3	🌴	WHARF		TRAIN STATION	
4			BUS STOP		
5	⛵				⛰

Travel to your destination, then catch the 12:20.

4

You reach the correct destination just in time to board the 12:20, which takes you to a tropical island. When you arrive, you find a sign congratulating you on your success so far.

On the sign below are a series of numbers and letters. You also find a map taped to the back of it. If you solved the previous puzzle, then you should hopefully have a good idea what the letters mean.

	A	B	C	D	E
1	MUSEUM	🌴			RESTAURANT
2					🌴
3			X		
4					
5	HOTEL		🌴		SWIMMING POOL

WELL DONE
LOCATION TRACKER!

2N 2SE 1SW 1S
2NW 2S 1NW 3N

You are at the "X" right now. Where should you go to next?

What do the numbers indicate? Do they have something to do with the distance to travel?

NEED THE SOLUTION? TURN TO PAGE 78

5

Another location, another challenge! You have been given this old-looking piece of paper with a couple of grids on it. The grid below looks like a map, but someone has drawn a letter in every square.

What a mess they have made! Worse still, on a second copy of the map, they have scribbled over some of the grid squares!

Perhaps there is a secret message here?

	A	B	C	D	E
1	A	G	O	A	L
2	M	O	T	T	O
3	A	T	H	E	M
4	G	L	O	B	E
5	A	C	H	E	S

Can you work out how to read it?

N
W   E
S

NEED A HINT? TURN TO PAGE 72

So now you know where to go, but the message is not precise. Luckily, there is another smaller grid, with some instructions written on it. Hopefully, they will tell you what to do next.

A3 – B2 – C1 – C2 – C3

B1 – ↙ – ↘

A3 – NE – NE – W

	A	B	C
1	!	T	A
2	H	O	R
3	B	E	D

What do you need to do when you get to the next destination?

You are on board, but now what? As you are thinking this, someone hands you a map and then disappears into a crowd of passengers.

Aha, this must tell you where to go next! But first, the boat will be docking at various ports. **At what time should you get off?**

Luckily, you have been given a clue. Some drawings scrawled on the bottom of the map tell you:

8

Now you know when to get off, you also need to work out where to go when you have disembarked! Taped behind the map you find two brief stories. Do you think they will help you work out where to go?

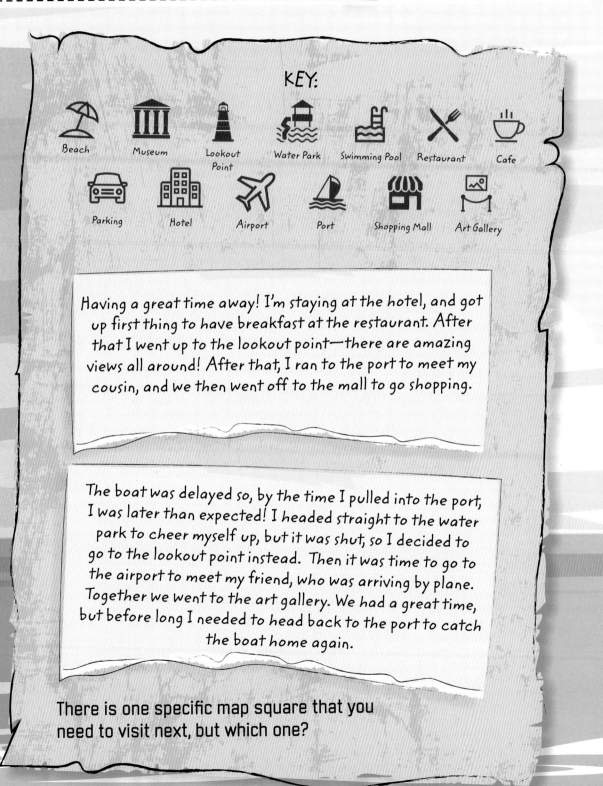

KEY:

Beach | Museum | Lookout Point | Water Park | Swimming Pool | Restaurant | Cafe

Parking | Hotel | Airport | Port | Shopping Mall | Art Gallery

Having a great time away! I'm staying at the hotel, and got up first thing to have breakfast at the restaurant. After that I went up to the lookout point—there are amazing views all around! After that, I ran to the port to meet my cousin, and we then went off to the mall to go shopping.

The boat was delayed so, by the time I pulled into the port, I was later than expected! I headed straight to the water park to cheer myself up, but it was shut, so I decided to go to the lookout point instead. Then it was time to go to the airport to meet my friend, who was arriving by plane. Together we went to the art gallery. We had a great time, but before long I needed to head back to the port to catch the boat home again.

There is one specific map square that you need to visit next, but which one?

NEED THE SOLUTION? TURN TO PAGE 78-79

After disembarking the boat, you head to the location indicated on the map, but it turns out to be a large place. You are not sure exactly where to go.

Just then, a picture appears on your phone. It was once a map, but letters have been written in most of the squares.

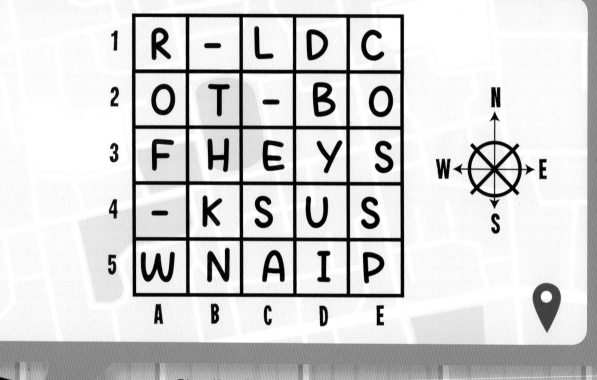

Shortly afterward, three text messages appear:

E1 - C5 - C1 - C1

D3 - E2 - D4 - A1

E1 - A2 - B5 - B2 - C5 - E1 - B2

UNKNOWN

Can you work out what the message means? What should you do now?

10

You follow the decoded instruction, but there is no answer. A few moments later, another text message arrives. This one contains a series of arrows. Surely they must represent another message but, if so, what exactly do they mean?

From C5 facing north:

There are only three types of arrow. Perhaps the straight ones mean to go straight on, while the other two mean to turn and face another direction?

NEED THE SOLUTION? TURN TO PAGE 79

11

You call again, and this time someone picks up. You ask to speak to the correct person, and they tell you that you must complete several challenges before the treasure's location is revealed!

Just as they hang up, you find an envelope with your name on it dropped on the floor. Inside are two logical puzzles. These must be the challenges!

First, can you work out how to complete this fence so that it joins all of the fence posts, and keeps the cows safely inside the field?

Hmm . . . it may help to first trace or copy these logical puzzles.

Some of the fence panels have already been placed, and you can only add new ones horizontally or vertically—not diagonally. The fence must be single loop, without any dead ends or sealed-off areas without cows.

For the second logical challenge, can you place four mirrors into the grid so that light shining directly into the grid from each shape is reflected onto the matching shape elsewhere?

There must be exactly one mirror per bold-lined area, and the mirrors must be placed diagonally either as / or \.

One mirror is already placed, to show you how it works. The light from some of the other shapes will need to reflect off multiple mirrors.

NEED THE SOLUTION? TURN TO PAGE 79

Just two more tasks and you will be finished! All that is left to do is to travel to a particular location and type in a three-digit number to unlock the treasure.

However, you don't yet know the three-digit number and all you have been given is the following scrap of paper, which you found in the same envelope as the logical puzzles:

B - Si - Ga - Sn - Ti
Bi - Te - As - N - O
Kr - Br - F - Ne - Rn - At

PERIODIC TABLE OF ELEMENTS

Whatever could it mean? You flick through your reference folder of codes and maps in case something useful catches your attention. Could something here be of help?

Now you just need to work out where to go! You have been given a map and some written directions, but can you trace the route correctly?

Enter the area shown on the map where the red arrow is, then head in the direction written in the instructions to avoid distractions or getting lost. **Follow the path correctly to find the location of the treasure.**

Take the first turning on the right-hand side, then keep going straight over the next junction before taking the next left. Keep going in the same direction until the road itself forces you to bend to the right, and follow it around the corner until the next junction. At this point, you should turn left, then left again at the end of that road, and keep going straight until you reach a main road. Now you should turn right before taking the first left. Keep going straight until you join another main road, then keep going in the same direction until you reach the end of the road. You are now in the right spot. Time to start digging for treasure!

NEED THE SOLUTION? TURN TO PAGE 79

CODE-BREAKER PUZZLE HINTS

Not sure how to solve a puzzle? Use these hints to help. Each puzzle has two hints. First read hint 1 and see if it helps. Read the second hint only if you still need help.

PUZZLE 1 (Page 4)

1. You are looking for parts of text that stand out from the rest. Are some parts highlighted in a particular way?

2. Read the words that have been highlighted.

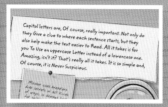

PUZZLE 2 (Page 5)

1. What does the very first sentence of the letter say?

2. Pay attention to every capital letter in the letter.

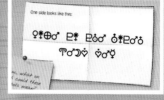

PUZZLE 3 (Page 6)

1. Each symbol represents one letter. The same symbol always represents the same letter.

2. The "M" of MOUTH is represented by the symbol "⊕."

PUZZLE 4 (Page 7)

1. Take a good look in the top left corner of the image side of the postcard.

2. If A=1, B=2, and C=3, what does D equal?

PUZZLE 5 (Page 8)

1. Each word needs to be replaced by the letter it represents in the Radiotelephony Spelling Alphabet.

2. You can also simply take the first letter of each word.

PUZZLE 6 (Page 9)

1. Each set of dots and dashes needs to be replaced by the letter it represents in the Morse code alphabet

2. Each line represents a different word.

PUZZLE 7 (Page 10)

1. The text "Can you follow what is going on" is a clue! The secret is to follow something.

2. Take a good look at the stamp, and the line that runs through it.

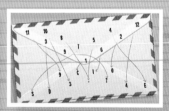

PUZZLE 8 (Page 11)

1. As the text suggests, the arrows need to be followed in a particular order. How would you normally arrange the numbers at the top?

2. Follow the arrow from "1," then from "2," from "3," and so on.

PUZZLE 9 (Page 12)

1. There are eight sentences in the letter, and eight words that you need to find.

2. Take one word from each sentence.

PUZZLE 10 (Page 13)

1. Pay special attention to the first word on the envelope.

2. That word is "Initially," and it is a hint to read all of the initial letters of the words.

PUZZLE 11 (Page 14)

1. You need to imagine replacing each empty square in one grid with the contents of the corresponding square in the other (tracing paper could be used to help).

2. This will create a five-word phrase.

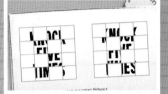

PUZZLE 12 (Page 15)

1. You need to imagine replacing each empty square in one grid with the contents of the corresponding square in the other (tracing paper could be used to help).

2. This will create a three-word phrase.

PUZZLE 13 (Page 16)

1. Imagine that each of the images consisted of four tiles that could be picked up and put back in a different order.

2. For the first picture, the top-left and bottom-right tiles are already in the correct position.

PUZZLE 14 (Page 17)

1. Imagine that each of the images consisted of four tiles that could be picked up and put back in a different order.

2. The three letters do not spell a word, and there are no vowels.

PUZZLE 15 (Page 18)

1. Pay special attention to the **bold parts** of the text from the newspaper.

2. The system to reverse is the alphabet, so A becomes Z while Z becomes A.

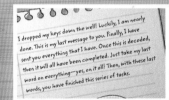

PUZZLE 16 (Page 19)

1. Pay particular attention to the sentence "Take my last word on everything—yes, on it all!"

2. You need to take the last word of every sentence.

SAFE-CRACKER HINTS

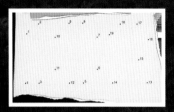

PUZZLE 1 (Page 20)

1. Does the picture with all the numbers remind you of something you have seen before?

2. It is a dot-to-dot puzzle. You should trace over the page, copy it, or try to solve it in your head by tracing with a finger and working out what the "picture" is.

PUZZLE 2 (Page 21)

1. Solve the maze, avoiding all dead ends and without backtracking on yourself.

2. Note which numbers you pass on your correct path through the maze.

PUZZLE 3 (Page 22)

1. Pay attention to the sketch at the bottom of the blackboard, which is important!

2. The grids on the sketch and on the paper both have seven columns and six rows.

PUZZLE 4 (Page 23)

1. Imagine yourself going through the maze. The three arrows correspond to the first three turns you would make.

2. Find the direct solution to the maze and make a list of all the turns you make from the entry arrow to the exit arrow.

PUZZLE 5 (Page 24)

1. Pay attention to the number code shown on the piano and sketched at the bottom of the page.

2: Looking at the numbering from 1 to 5. Which notes do you think would symbolize 6 to 9?

PUZZLE 6 (Page 25)

1. Compare the appearance of the six dice faces on the shelf with the incomplete faces on the dials.

2. Remember that the dice faces can be rotated, so the 2, 3, and 6 faces could look different from the examples.

PUZZLE 7 (Page 26)

1. Does this grid of numbers remind you of a type of puzzle you have seen before?

2. It is a word search grid, except it contains numbers instead of words. Find the listed numbers written in any direction on the grid, including diagonally and backward.

PUZZLE 8 (Page 27)

1. Treat each box as containing a series of mathematical instructions, which reading them from top to bottom.

2. In the first box, start with 17 and then multiply by 2, before then subtracting 7, and so on.

PUZZLE 9 (Page 28)

1. Count the number of boxes making up each group, from A to D.

2. None of the boxes can be floating in the air.

PUZZLE 10 (Page 29)

1. In a sudoku puzzle, a number cannot repeat in a row, column, or within a bold-lined box.

2. In the first grid, the red-circled square cannot contain a 3 or 4, because they are already in that row, and it cannot contain a 1, because there is one in that bold-lined box, so it must contain a 2.

PUZZLE 11 (Page 30)

1. You need to find the odd image in each frame, allowing for the fact that some of the images are rotated differently.

2. The differences are very subtle, so look carefully at small details.

PUZZLE 12 (Page 31)

1. There are four bars on the model and four holes in the clear box.

2. What would happen if you dropped the model into the box, so that the four bars went through the four holes?

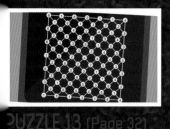

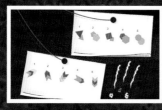

PUZZLE 13 (Page 32)

1. The path has been labeled straightforwardly, but it is a little hard to find, and is not in a straight line.

2. The path travels from 1 to 2, then to 3, 4, 5, and

PUZZLE 14 (Page 33)

1. There is one image in each row of five that does not fit in with the others.

2. In the first row, one of the images has a different number of sides to all the others.

PUZZLE 15 (Page 34)

1. Each letter represents a different feature of the picture it is next to.

2. In the first puzzle, an "S" as the first letter indicates a star pointing up, while a

PUZZLE 16 (Page 35)

1. Can you find the star hidden inside any of the four square images below it?

2. You can find the star in one of the images, but it has been rotated to make it

TECH DECODER HINTS

PUZZLE 1 (Page 36)

1. Can you spot the differences between the two log-in screens?

2. Find the words that are different on the second login screen.

PUZZLE 2 (Page 37)

1. Pay attention to the ASCII letter codes shown in the background.

2. Replace each of the numbers in the identification key attempt with its corresponding ASCII letter.

PUZZLE 3 (Page 38)

1. Take a look at the keypad on the phone.

2. There are three "5"s together on the first row, so what letter corresponds to pressing the "5" key three times on the phone?

PUZZLE 4 (Page 39)

1. Did you notice the calculator on the page? This is a hint!

2. The response to "BREAKFAST" is "EGGSHELL." Can you see why? Try looking at things from a different perspective.

PUZZLE 5 (Page 40)

1. You don't need to make sense of the computer code, but there are certain plain English parts that you need to read.

2. In particular, read the second line of the code, which says "Pay attention to the /*...*/."

PUZZLE 6 (Page 41)

1. One in each pair is a decoy, so you need only one letter from each pair.

2. In the first row, take the T and the O to spell "TO."

PUZZLE 7 (Page 42)

1. Does anything in the party invite 'stand out to you'?

2. Read only the words that have been made to stand out in some way, such as by being underlined, for example.

PUZZLE 8 (Page 43)

1. Look for the differences in the second file when compared to the first.

2. Read only the letters that have changed in the second file.

PUZZLE 9 (Page 44)

1. You need to be "shifty" like the gang to solve this puzzle, by shifting the letters about so A becomes B, B becomes C, and so on.

2. Carry on in a similar manner, replacing C with D, D with E, and so on, until you replace Z with A.

PUZZLE 10 (Page 45)

1. To solve this puzzle, it will really help to have solved the previous puzzle.

2. The solution to the previous puzzle tells you exactly how to solve this one, by shifting each letter a certain number of spaces through the alphabet.

PUZZLE 11 (Page 46)

1. The numbers in the "index" are just like the index of a book. So what might they be indexing by, if it is not by page number?

2. The index numbers equal the number of words in each sentence, so read the tenth word on the first row.

PUZZLE 12 (Page 47)

1. This code is similar to the previous one, except that it is no longer indexing by word.

2. This code indexes by letters instead, so 1 refers to the first letter in the word, 2 is the second letter, and so on.

PUZZLE 13 (Page 48)

1. If you "alphabetize" something, you sort it into alphabetical order.

2. Arrange the letters on each row into alphabetical order to make a word. The first row becomes "ACCESS."

PUZZLE 14 (Page 49)

1. You are looking for a door access code, so what might each jumbled line turn into?

2. Each line contains jumbled-up letters that spell out a number.

PUZZLE 15 (Page 50)

1. There are some letters missing from each of the lines.

2. Make a note of all the missing letters, and then read them as one word per paragraph.

PUZZLE 16 (Page 51)

1. Why is "First" in italics in the first line of the document?

2. You need to take the "first" of something in each line.

LOCATION TRACKER HINTS

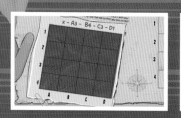

PUZZLE 1 (Page 52)

1. Start at the "X" in square A3, then trace a path to the next coordinate, B4.

2. Then, trace a path from B4 to C3, and finally to D1. What symbol does it make?

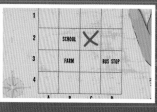

PUZZLE 2 (Page 53)

1. Treat each arrow as a separate instruction, requiring you to move one square in the direction shown.

2. Start at the "X" and move down one square, then down another square, then left one square, and so on.

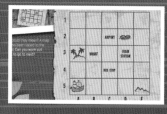

PUZZLE 3 (Page 54)

1. Notice that there is a compass shown on the page, so you know which way is north (N), east (E), south (S), and west (W).

2. Starting from the solution to Puzzle 2, follow the sequence of directions, moving one square in the given direction at each step.

PUZZLE 4 (Page 55)

1. Why are there now two compass directions in a single instruction, and what are the numbers for?

2: Where there are two compass directions together, you should move diagonally. The numbers show you how many squares to move in the given direction.

PUZZLE 5 (Page 56)

1. Why are there two copies of the map?

2. Why have some of the grid squares been scribbled out on one copy of the map, and how do they correspond to the letters?

PUZZLE 6 (Page 57)

1. This puzzle combines three codes from previous puzzles in this section.

2. The first line is similar to Puzzle 1, the second line is similar to Puzzle 2, and the third line is similar to Puzzle 5.

PUZZLE 7 (Page 58)

1. Each set of symbols will make a single digit, so once you have all three, you will have a time for a digital clock (X:YZ).

2: The dashes (-) join each symbol together in a row, so what would you see if you also joined them together in the same order on the map?

PUZZLE 8 (Page 59)

1. The places referred to in the stories can be found on the map, but you will need to use the key to work out which symbol represents which place.

2. Try tracing a route for the places visited in each story.

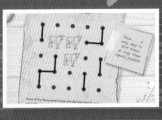
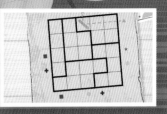

PUZZLE 9 (Page 60)

1. This puzzle might appear similar to a previous one, but notice that the coordinates are not joined by lines this time, and the squares indicated are not always next to one another.

2. Read the letters found in all of the indicated squares.

PUZZLE 10 (Page 61)

1. The curved arrows indicate a change of direction, but not movement.

2. Keep track of which direction you are facing, and that the straight arrows move you one step in that direction.

PUZZLE 11 (Page 62)

1. There is a single loop visiting every post, which means that every post must have exactly two fence panels connected to it.

2. This means that in each of the corners you can place two fence panels immediately, since diagonal fence panels are not allowed.

PUZZLE 12 (Page 63)

1. There are four bold-lined areas without mirrors, so you need to place four more mirrors into the grid.

2. Start by placing a mirror so that the two stars can see each other—there is only one square where this can fit.

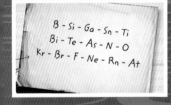

PUZZLE 13 (Page 64)

1. The dashes (-) between the letters are similar to those in previous codes, which indicated that you should join things together.

2. Find these letters, or letter pairs, on the copy of the periodic table that is shown on the page.

PUZZLE 14 (Page 65)

1. You will find this easier if you trace the route with the non-writing end of a pen or pencil, because your finger may obscure the smaller roads.

2. If you struggle to trace the route, take a look at the solution and work out how the description of the route corresponds to the path that is shown.

CODE-BREAKER SOLUTIONS

Most of the puzzles are explained in greater detail within the hints section (pages 66–73), and only the end solution or any missing information is given here. To see how to reach a solution given below, you should first read the hints for that puzzle.

PUZZLE 1 (Page 4)

Read the highlighted words to reveal: "YOU HAVE SOLVED THE FIRST CODE"

PUZZLE 2 (Page 5)

Put all the capital letters together to reveal: "CONGRATULATIONS?"

PUZZLE 3 (Page 6)

The paper reads: "COME TO THE HOTEL" and "WEAR RED"

PUZZLE 4 (Page 7)

The numbers decode to: "YOUR CONTACT IS JAMES"

PUZZLE 5 (Page 8)

The message reads: "LISTEN FOR SECRETS"

PUZZLE 6 (Page 9)

The Morse code decodes to: "MORSE CODE CAN DRIVE YOU DOTTY"

PUZZLE 7 (Page 10)

Reading along the line, starting from the outside of the stamp, the message is: "PARCEL TOMORROW"

PUZZLE 8 (Page 11)

Reading the bottom line in the order pointed at by the arrows, the message reads: "CODE-IS-7394"

PUZZLE 9 (Page 12)

The first words of each sentence can be read together to reveal the hidden message: "I WILL NEVER USE THE SAME CODE TWICE"

PUZZLE 10 (Page 13)

Take the initial letter of each word to form one new word per line, reading: "I WILL ARRIVE TONIGHT"

PUZZLE 11 (Page 14)

Replacing the empty squares in one grid with those from the other reveals the message: "PLAY SOME LOUD POP SONGS"

PUZZLE 12 (Page 15)

Replacing the empty squares in one grid with those from the other reveals the message: "KNOCK FIVE TIMES"

PUZZLE 13 (Page 16)

Imagine rearranging the tiles in each image to reveal the code: 372

PUZZLE 14 (Page 17)

Imagine rearranging the tiles in each image to reveal the code: QMS

PUZZLE 15 (Page 18)

Replace A with Z, B with Y, C with X, and so on to reveal the message: "CONGRATULATIONS, FRIEND! YOU ARE NEARLY THERE. JUST ONE FINAL TASK REMAINS."

PUZZLE 16 (Page 19)

Take the last word of every sentence to reveal the hidden message: "WELL DONE. YOU HAVE COMPLETED ALL TASKS."

SAFE-CRACKER SOLUTIONS

PUZZLE 1 (Page 20)

Imagine joining the dots to create a "picture" of three digits: 102

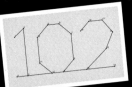

PUZZLE 2 (Page 21)

The direct route through the maze passes over five digits, creating the number: 75982

PUZZLE 3 (Page 22)

The words in the grid correspond to the shaded boxes in the sketch to reveal:
"THE SECRET CODE THAT YOU NEED IS FOUR THREE SEVEN" The three-digit code you need is 437

PUZZLE 4 (Page 23)

The direct route through the maze makes 14 turns: *left, right, right, left, right, left, right, left, left, right, right, left, left, right.* So, the safe dial needs to be turned:

One to the left, two to the right, one to the left, one to the right, one to the left, one to the right, two to the left, two to the right, two to the left, one to the right—phew!

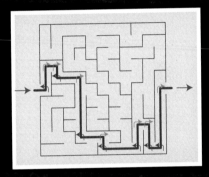

PUZZLE 5 (Page 24)

By extending the musical note code shown on the piano to the higher notes, the safe door code can be read as: 5793

PUZZLE 6 (Page 25)

The missing faces must be: 5, 6, 6 (with the face with six dots being at a different rotation on the second and third dice).

PUZZLE 7 (Page 26)

All but one of the numbers can be found in the grid, solving it like a standard word search puzzle; the number that cannot be found, so is different to all the others, is: 629479

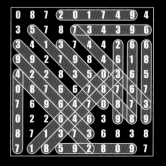

PUZZLE 8 ((Page 27)

Follow each chain of mathematical instructions from top to bottom, resulting in values of 61, 19, 9 and 3. So the 6-digit code is: 611993

17	34	27	45	41	61
12	3	18	17	34	19
14	22	11	8	27	9
20	11	29	19	12	3

PUZZLE 9 (Page 28)

Count the number of boxes in each group, assuming that none of them are floating in the air, to give totals of:
A=10, B=11, C=15 and D=11

PUZZLE 10 (Page 29)

The solutions to the circled sudoku squares reveals the code: 211

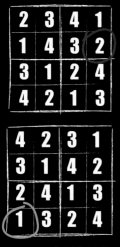

PUZZLE 11 (Page 30)

The odd ones out are, in the order of diamonds, keys, padlocks: 2, 2, 6

PUZZLE 12 (Page 31)

Imagine inserting the piece with four bars into the four holes on the top of the box, hiding some of the letters to reveal: RHINO

PUZZLE 13 (Page 32)

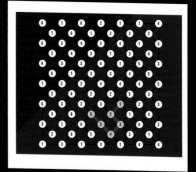

PUZZLE 14 (Page 33)

Each set of images contains one odd image out:

- In the first set, image 4 is the only one with five sides.

- In the second set, image 5 is the only one with the smaller shape in front of the larger shape.

- In the third set, image 1 is the only one where the sections get larger toward the tip of the arrow, as opposed to the tail.

So, the code is: 451

PUZZLE 15 (Page 34)

In each puzzle, each letter represents a different feature of the image it is next to as follows:

First puzzle:
S = star points up
Z = star points down
O = yellow star
R = blue star
B = white hexagon
F = pink hexagon

Second puzzle:
Q = green oval
M = orange oval
L = blue circle
A = pink circle
P = oval in front
C = oval behind

Third puzzle:
N = large yellow triangle
B = large red triangle
G = small purple triangle
H = small green triangle
Y = small triangle top
W = small triangle bottom right
O = small triangle bottom left

So, the solutions are ZOF, QLC, and BGW, in turn, which makes the code: 324

PUZZLE 16 (Page 35)

Find each of the smaller images inside one of the four larger images to reveal the code: 243

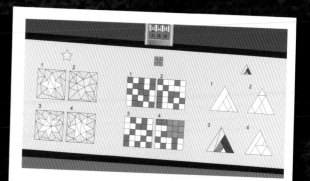

TECH DECODER SOLUTIONS

PUZZLE 1 (Page 36)

The words that differ on the second log-in screen make the message:
"THE LOG-IN PASSWORD IS 'ASSIGNMENT'"

PUZZLE 2 (Page 37)

Replace each of the seven two-digit numbers in the incorrect log-in attempt with its corresponding ASCII letter from the code table to spell out: "LETMEIN"

PUZZLE 3 (Page 38)

The numbers correspond to the same buttons on the phone keypad. A number appearing once indicates the first letter on that button, a number appearing twice indicates the second letter, and so on. So, with one word per line, the message decodes to:
"ALWAYS USE A VOICE ENCODER"

PUZZLE 4 (Page 39)

Read each response upside down, as indicated by the upside-down calculator screen showing HELLO (07734), to give the responses:
"EGGSHELL," "SLEIGH," "GOGGLES," and "GLOBE"

PUZZLE 5 (Page 40)

Read only the text between the "/*" and "*/" markers, as requested by the second line of the code, to reveal: "WHENEVER ACCESSING OUR COMPUTER SYSTEMS REMEMBER TO OPEN OUR IDENTIFICATION SOFTWARE SO THAT WE CAN TRACK ALL LEGITIMATE LOGINS"

PUZZLE 6 (Page 41)

Delete one "decoy" letter from each pair to leave:
"TO IDENTIFY YOURSELF, TYPE IN CUCUMBER"

PUZZLE 7 (Page 42)

Read only the bold, italic, and underlined words to reveal: "OUR NEW HEADQUARTERS IS IN PARIS"

PUZZLE 8 (Page 43)

The changed letters on the second invitation spell out:
"DO NOT ATTEND THE PARTY"

PUZZLE 9 (Page 44)

Shift each letter one place to the right in the alphabet, with Z becoming A, to reveal: "TO READ THE NEXT CODE, SHIFT BY THIRTEEN PLACES THROUGH THE ALPHABET"

PUZZLE 10 (Page 45)

Shift each letter 13 places to the right (or left) in the alphabet to reveal:
"THE POLICE ARE WATCHING US. ALWAYS TURN OFF YOUR MACHINE WHEN YOU LEAVE THE OFFICE"

PUZZLE 11 (Page 46)

Each index number indicates which word to read. For example, in row 1 we select word 10, which is "Main." The overall message reads: "MAIN SERVER NOW LOCATED IN FRANKFURT"

PUZZLE 12 (Page 47)

Each index number indicated a letter in the word, so 1 is the first letter, 2 is the second, and so on. The overall message is: "DAFFODIL"

PUZZLE 13 (Page 48)

Rearrange the letters on each row into alphabetical order to spell out:
"ACCESS DOOR IS

PUZZLE 14 (Page 49)

Rearrange the letters on each line to spell the "THREE," "NINE," "SEVEN, "FIVE," "EIGHT," and "ZERO." So, the door

PUZZLE 15 (Page 50)

Nine words are missing a letter, and these letters spell out, with one word per paragraph:

PUZZLE 16 (Page 51)

Reading only the first letters of each line spells out, with one word per paragraph:
"WE HAVE ESCAPED"

LOCATION TRACKER SOLUTIONS

PUZZLE 1 (Page 52)

Joining the squares indicated by the coordinates in the order given reveals a CHECK or TICK shape.

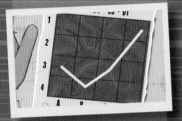

PUZZLE 2 (Page 53)

Moving one square in the direction shown by each arrow in turn, you will arrive at the BUS STOP.

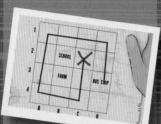

PUZZLE 3 (Page 54)

Starting at the bus stop (as instructed in the previous puzzle), follow the directions, moving "south" one square for "S," "east" one square for "E," and so on. You will reach the AIRPORT.

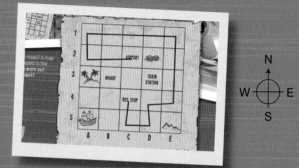

PUZZLE 4 (Page 55)

Follow the directions as in the previous puzzle, but moving diagonally where there are two compass points, such as NE to move up and to the right. The numbers show how many squares to move in the given direction. The correct path will lead you to the MUSEUM.

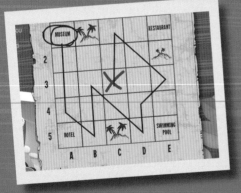

PUZZLE 5 (Page 56)

Ignore the letters in squares on the first map that correspond to squares that have been scribbled out on the second map to reveal: "GO TO THE BEACH"

PUZZLE 6 (Page 57)

Follow the coordinates across the grid to spell out one word per line. The secret message is: "BOARD THE BOAT"

PUZZLE 7 (Page 58)

Note the watch showing X:YZ, and then the series of symbols for each letter. Join them together, in the order shown, to trace a path that makes the shape of a digit, revealing the time: 7:40

PUZZLE 8 (Page 59)

Use the key to find each of the symbols corresponding to the places visited in each story, and trace a path that joins them in the order encountered in the story to reveal: "2B"

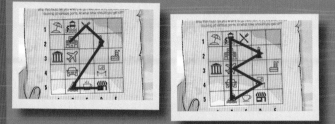

PUZZLE 9 (Page 60)

Read the letters in the indicated map squares to reveal a message, with one word per row of coordinates, reading: "CALL YOUR CONTACT"

PUZZLE 10 (Page 61)

Follow the arrow instructions, changing direction for the curved arrows and moving forward one square for each straight arrow, to spell out the message: "ASK-FOR-THE-BOSS"

PUZZLE 11 (Page 62)

Place the panels as shown in the picture below:

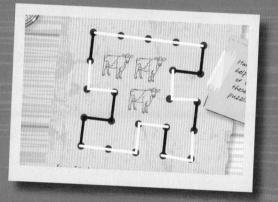

PUZZLE 12 (Page 63)

Place the mirrors as shown in the picture below:

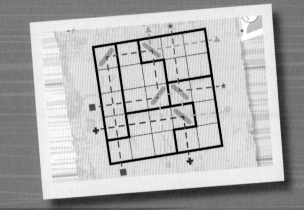

PUZZLE 13 (Page 64)

Trace each of the three sequences of letters and letter pairs on the periodic table to reveal: 359

PUZZLE 14 (Page 65)

Follow the directions to take the route shown below:

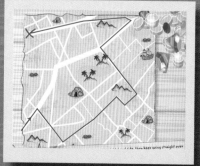

ABOUT THE AUTHOR

Dr. Gareth Moore is the best-selling author of a wide range of puzzle and brain-training books for both kids and adults, including *The Mammoth Book of Brain Games* and *Brain Games for Clever Kids*. He is also founder of the daily brain training site www.BrainedUp.com. He gained his Ph.D from Cambridge University (UK) in the field of computer speech recognition, teaching machines to understand spoken words.

First published in 2023 by Hungry Tomato Ltd
F15, Old Bakery Studios, Blewetts Wharf, Malpas Road, Truro, Cornwall, TR1 1QH, UK.

Text and puzzles copyright © 2023 Dr. Gareth Moore

Copyright © 2023 Hungry Tomato Ltd

Thanks to the creative team:
Senior editor: Anna Hussey
Graphic Designer: Amy Harvey

A CIP catalogue record for this book is available from the British Library.

ISBN 978-1-914087-67-7

Printed in China

Discover more at
www.hungrytomato.com

Check out other Beetle Books by Dr. Gareth Moore: